MW01514598

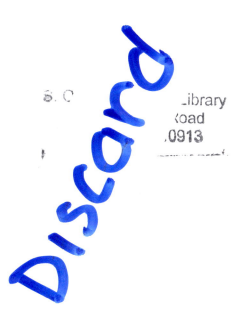

B. C   Library
                        Road
                        0913

Benjamin Franklin

Heroes of the American Revolution

★

Don McLeese

SOUTH ORANGETOWN MIDDLE SCHOOL

24399

Benjamin Franklin

B FRA

Rourke
Publishing LLC
Vero Beach, Florida 32964

© 2005 Rourke Publishing LLC

All rights reserved. No part of this book may be reproduced or utilized in any form or by any means, electronic or mechanical including photocopying, recording, or by any information storage and retrieval system without permission in writing from the publisher.

www.rourkepublishing.com

PHOTO CREDITS: Cover Portrait, Title page, Pages 4, 6, 20, 23, 24,from the Library of Congress;Cover Scene, Pages 5, 9, 13, 17, 18, 19, 27, 29 ©North Wind Picture Archives; Pages 10, 14 © Getty Images

Title page: *A portrait of Benjamin Franklin*

Editor: Frank Sloan

Cover and page design by Nicola Stratford

Library of Congress Cataloging-in-Publication Data

McLeese, Don.
  Benjamin Franklin / Don McLeese.
     p. cm. -- (Heroes of the American revolution)
  Includes bibliographical references and index.
   ISBN 1-59515-216-4 (hardcover)
 1. Franklin, Benjamin, 1706-1790--Juvenile literature. 2. Statesmen--United States--Biography--Juvenile literature. 3. Scientists--United States--Biography--Juvenile literature. 4. Inventors--United States--Biography--Juvenile literature. 5. Printers--United States--Biography--Juvenile literature. I. Title.
E302.6.F8M455 2004
973.3'092--dc22

                                    2004007601

Printed in the USA

LB/LB

Table of Contents

★

An Amazing Man

Benjamin Franklin was one of the most amazing men who ever lived in America. Few people have done as many things as well as Benjamin did. He was so

important in helping the United States become its own country during the Revolutionary War era that Thomas Jefferson called him "the greatest man . . . of the age and country in which he lived."

Benjamin Franklin L.L.D.

The Declaration of Independence is signed. Franklin is seated at the right.

Franklin is greeted by his family when he returns from Europe to his Philadelphia home.

Benjamin Franklin never became president like Jefferson did, and he wasn't a great army general like George Washington. Instead, Franklin served his country by dealing with other countries, getting France to be on America's side in the battle of **independence** from England.

He also traveled to England to help make the peace that ended the war and made the United States of America its own country.

Benjamin Franklin was a great **diplomat**. He was also great as a writer, scientist, inventor, and printer of books. Few people can become great at so many different things, but few people were as special as the amazing Benjamin Franklin.

A Big Family

⭐

Benjamin was born on January 17, 1706. He was the 15th child of father Josiah and mother Abiah Franklin. He was the youngest of ten sons in a family of 17. The family lived in Boston.

MAKING SOAP AND CANDLES

Benjamin's family made soap and candles in a shop. They stirred the ingredients in a big cooking pot, called a vat, and then shaped them as they got cooler and harder.

~

Both Josiah and Abiah needed to work very hard with a family that big. Josiah had a shop where he made soap and candles. Abiah took care of the house and the children. The Franklins didn't have much money, because they spent all they had to feed that many people.

A view of Franklin's birthplace in Boston

Young Benjamin Franklin spent time as a candle maker.

Leaving School

Benjamin went to school for just two years. He learned to love books, and he was very good at reading, writing, and arithmetic. But his poor family didn't have enough money to keep Ben and the rest of his sisters and brothers in school.

So Ben quit school at the age of ten. He went to work helping his father make soap and candles. He worked as many as 12 to 14 hours a day. Ben didn't mind helping his father, but he knew that he wanted to do more with his life than make candles.

BEN OR BENJAMIN?

"Benjamin" was Franklin's full and proper first name, but a lot of people called him by his nickname, "Ben."

~

Becoming a Printer

★

When Benjamin was 12, he quit working with his father in the candle shop. He wanted to become a printer, like his older brother James. A printer uses a machine called a printing press to print books, magazines, or newspapers. James agreed to let Ben work with him and learn to become a printer.

A look at one of Franklin's printing presses

Ben Franklin visits his brother's printing office.

While he was working with James, Ben also did some writing. He wrote articles for a newspaper for James to print. But he didn't sign his own name, because he didn't think James would print them if he knew they came from his own brother.

S. Orangetown MS Library
160 Van Wyck Road
Blauvelt, NY 10913

APPRENTICE

When someone like Ben is learning a new job, he is called an **apprentice**. An apprentice makes little or no money while he's learning, but eventually develops the skills to do the job himself. Ben was a printer's apprentice before he became a printer.

Moving to Philadelphia

★

In 1723, when he was 17, Ben quit working for James and moved to Philadelphia. This was the largest city in America at the time. Ben would continue to live there for most of his long life. He became the most famous person in that city. He was called "the first citizen of Philadelphia."

MARRIAGE

In 1730, Ben married Deborah Read Rogers. They had two sons within two years and a daughter ten years later.

~

For five years, Franklin worked for other printers. In 1728, he became part owner of a print shop. He printed a newspaper called *The Pennsylvania Gazette*, which became one of the best in America. He also wrote many of the articles for it. Franklin published this famous newspaper from 1729 until 1766.

Franklin demonstrates his printing press in Philadelphia.

Poor Richard

As a writer and publisher, Franklin had even more success with *Poor Richard's Almanack*, which he put out every year from 1733 until 1758. Included within the **almanac** were sayings written by Benjamin as "Poor Richard." These offered advice on how to become successful by working hard and being good.

Some of the best known sayings are "Early to bed and early to rise/Makes a man healthy, wealthy, and wise" and "God helps them that help themselves."

The title page of Poor Richard's Almanack, *1733*

ALMANAC

An almanac is a book that comes out once a year. In those days, the word was sometimes spelled "almanack." Often the book tells things about the year to come, such as what the weather will be like and lists of facts from the previous year.

~

A portrait of Ben Franklin working in his office

Benjamin experiments with his kite.

Important Scientist and Inventor

During this period, Franklin became one of the first scientists to experiment with electricity. He conducted his most famous experiment in 1752. He flew a homemade kite in a thunderstorm. When it was struck by lightning, he proved that lightning is a form of electricity, and that people could control its power.

As an inventor, Franklin developed the most popular stove of his day, called the Franklin stove, and **bifocal** eyeglasses, which are still used today.

Serving His Country

★

Though his writing and his inventions made Benjamin Franklin a great American, it was his service to the government that made him one of the greatest of all. Like the other Founding Fathers of this country, he believed that America should start its own country instead of being ruled by England.

Because Franklin was known as such a smart and great man, he was sent to England in 1757 to tell America's side of the story. Except for a period of time between 1762 and 1764, he lived in England until 1775. When the Revolutionary War began between England and America, Benjamin Franklin returned home to Philadelphia.

FOUNDING FATHERS

We often refer to those who were most important in starting this country as the "Founding Fathers." Along with George Washington, Thomas Jefferson, and John Adams, Benjamin Franklin was one of most respected.

~

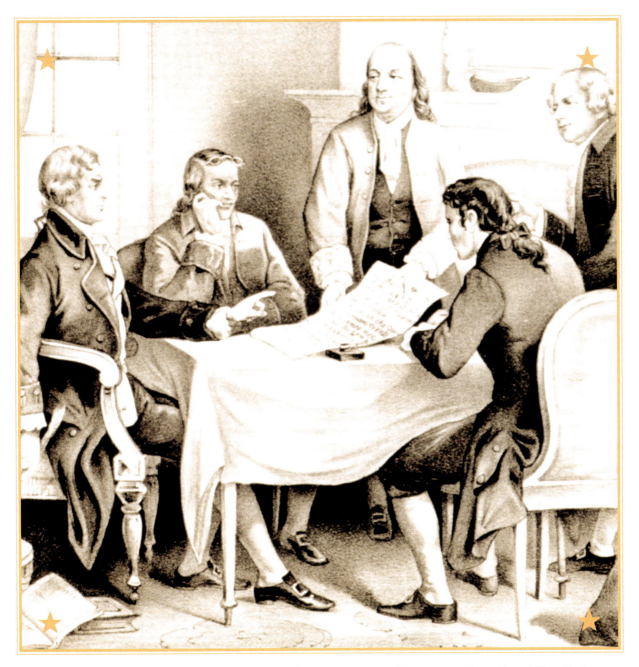

A committee made up of Thomas Jefferson, Roger Sherman, Ben Franklin, Robert Livingston, and John Adams. Together they worked on the Declaration of Independence.

A reception given for Franklin during his time in France

The Great Statesman

When America was preparing its Declaration of Independence from England in 1776, Benjamin Franklin put a lot of his ideas into it. He then went to France later that year and helped convince that country to take the side of America rather than helping England. France sent money and support to help the American cause.

If Franklin hadn't been able to talk France into taking America's side, many believe that England would have won. Benjamin Franklin helped write the treaty that put France on America's side in 1778. He also wrote the Treaty of Paris that ended the war in 1783.

Franklin also helped write the Constitution in 1787, which established the government of the new country. He was the only Founding Father to sign and help write all four of the important papers that made this a new country: the Declaration of Independence, the Constitution, and the two treaties.

TREATY

A written agreement between two countries is often called a treaty. Countries have representatives sign treaties when they agree to be on the same side against another country, or when they decide to stop fighting a war.

Franklin and Alexander Hamilton discuss the framing of the Constitution.

A Long, Full Life

Benjamin Franklin lived so long and did so much that it almost seems like he had more than one life. As a successful printer, he went from being a poor boy to becoming a rich man. He was able to sell his printing business and retire from it when he was only 42 years old.

When Benjamin Franklin died in Philadelphia on April 17, 1790, he was so beloved that 20,000 people showed up to honor him at his funeral.

Franklin devoted the second half of his life to public service. He lived another 42 years and spent most of this time as one of the greatest American **statesmen**. He went to other countries to tell why America should be its own country, and he helped the United States of America develop its new government.

The elderly Franklin is shown with his grandsons during a trip to Paris.

Time Line

1706	★ Franklin is born.
1723	★ Franklin moves to Philadelphia.
1728	★ Franklin becomes part owner of a print shop.
1730	★ Franklin marries Deborah Read Rogers.
1752	★ Franklin conducts his most famous experiment, proving lightning is a form of electricity.
1757	★ Franklin is sent to live in England.
1776	★ America issues its Declaration of Independence from England.
1787	★ Franklin helps to write and signs the Constitution.
1790	★ Franklin dies.

Glossary

almanac (OL muh NAK) — an annual publication with a lot of information for the given year

apprentice (uh PRENT us) — a beginner, someone who is learning a job

bifocal (BY FO cul) — eyeglasses that have one part of the lens to help see things that are close and another part of the lens to help see things far away

diplomat (DUP luh MAT) — someone who serves his or her country in dealing with another country

independence (IN duh PEN dunts) — freedom from another government

statesmen (STAYTS mun) — men who serve as national leaders but are not necessarily elected to office

Index

Further Reading

Burke, Rick. *Benjamin Franklin.* Heinemann Library, 2003

Fleming, Candace. *Ben Franklin's Almanac: Being a True Account of the Good Gentleman's Life.* Simon & Schuster, 2003

Glass, Maya. *Benjamin Franklin: Early American Genius.* The Rosen Publishing Group, 2003

Websites to Visit

http://www.colonialhall.com/franklin/franklin.asp

http://library.thinkquest.org/22254/home.htm

http://odur.let.rug.nl/~usa/B/bfranklin/franklin.htm

About the Author

Don McLeese is an award-winning journalist whose work has appeared in many newspapers and magazines. He earned his M.A. degree in English from the University of Chicago, taught feature writing at the University of Texas and has frequently contributed to the World Book Encyclopedia. He lives with his wife and two daughters in West Des Moines, Iowa.